HOW TO GROW YOUR WEALTH THROUGH TAX PLANNING

How to Grow Your Wealth Through Tax Planning

CHARLENE QUAH

XQ CPA

For Andre,

With deep gratitude for your endless support over the years, especially through the most difficult times. Your presence has meant more than words can express.

For Mom,

You have always been my strongest supporter. Your unconditional love and unwavering support have given me the strength to persist through tough times.

CONTENTS

PREFACE: WHY DID YOU START YOUR BUSINESS?

Based on the Small Business Statistics of 2024 Compiled by Forbes[1]*:*

- 99.9% of businesses across the US are small businesses.
- Nearly half of all US employees are employed by a small business.
- Out of the 33.2 million small businesses, 27.1 million are run by a single owner and have no employees.

If you own your own business and have been running it for a while, you will agree that running your own business is not an easy thing to do. Not only do you work long hours, but you are also constantly under the pressure of having to live with the uncertainty that comes with owning your own business.

So why did you start your own business? Why are you putting in constant hours to make it successful? Because you believe that running your own business will get you closer to achieving your dream! You believe that running your own business will give you the opportunity to change the world by providing better services or products to the people you choose to serve.

Hence, your business was not created by accident. Your business was created because of your intention, followed by **careful and strategic planning and execution**.

If you own a profitable business and have been running it for quite some time, you will agree that your tax bill is probably always the largest expense in your business.

Hence, when searching for a CPA to work with, most business owners have the expectation that their CPA should help them reduce their tax burden. The problem here is that many business owners fail to realize that **tax preparation is NOT tax planning**.

Tax preparation happens after the fact. It happens after the tax year, which ends on December 31st of every calendar year. The due date of most business tax returns falls on March 15th and the due date of ALL individual tax returns falls on April 15th.

If your expectation is that a CPA should be able to apply some magic wand to reduce your tax bill after December 31st, you are most likely missing out on LOTS of opportunities to greatly reduce your taxes. To reduce your tax burden effectively, you need proper tax planning.

Most of the time, business owners perceive tax planning as merely implementing a few tips to cut their tax bills. The reality is that successful tax planning requires **careful and strategic planning and execution**, just like the approach you have taken to start, grow, and maintain your business.

It is true that your CPA plays an important role in guiding you and giving you the right advice and the right tax strategies. However, without a proper implementation and monitoring system, tax planning becomes less effective. You will only scratch the surface without truly benefiting from the real value of what tax planning can bring to you and your business.

WHY TAX PLANNING? THE XQ CPA METHODOLOGY

"The U.S. income tax system is based on the idea of **voluntary compliance**. Under this system, it is the taxpayer's responsibility to report all income. **Tax evasion** is illegal. One way that people try to evade paying taxes is by failing to report all or some of their income. Sometimes people do not report income gained through illegal activities such as gambling and selling stolen goods. Other times they do not report all the tips they collect or the money they earn through legal activities such as garage sales, baby-sitting, tutoring, or yard work. Such money-making activities are part of the **underground economy**, which exists as a way to avoid paying taxes. If taxpayers fail to pay what officials say they owe, the IRS can assess a penalty, in addition to collecting the back taxes.

In contrast, **tax avoidance** is perfectly legal. IRS regulations allow eligible taxpayers to claim certain deductions, credits, and adjustments to income. For instance, some homeowners can claim a deduction for interest they pay on a home mortgage. Working parents may be able to claim a credit for child-care expenses. There are also deductions based on the number of family members. These are only a few of the many ways people can legally limit the tax they pay. However, the taxpayer must be able to prove that he or she qualifies. Many people pay more federal income tax than necessary because they misunderstand tax laws and fail to keep good records."[2]

Tax planning is a process that you put in place in your business to enable you to avoid overpaying taxes.

Why Tax Planning?

Tax planning is important for every business because **proper tax planning encourages tax avoidance LEGALLY.**

Tax Planning 360, The XQ CPA Methodology

The journey of tax planning begins with you understanding your tax position and then identifying the right strategies that are most effective for you and your business. To practice implementing effective tax strategies, you need to know HOW to apply them.

Tax Planning is Not All About Spending Money:

At the end of the day, successful tax planning is not just about buying a few pieces of equipment. Successful tax implementation challenges a business owner's ability to think deductibly i. e. how do you maximize your business deductions by justifying that these activities are directly related to the ordinary and necessary part of your business operations?

Below, I've provided an overview of XQ CPA's Tax Planning Methodology. I've broken down the whole process into three phases:

1. **Understand Your Tax Situation and Set Your Tax Goal**
2. **Strategy Selection, Tax Allocation, and Implementation**
3. **Strategy Evaluation and Final Tax Balance Determination**

Below, I have outlined a step-by-step approach for each phase to guide you through the tax planning process.

Phase I - Understand Your Tax Situation and Set Your Tax Goal

Tax planning starts here. For a business owner, the key to successful tax planning lies in the groundwork laid beforehand.

Before diving into specific tax strategies, it's

crucial to follow these initial steps: ensure your financial statements are accurate, assess your current tax position based on your financial performance, and clearly define your desired tax outcome. Once you have a solid understanding of these factors, you'll be ready to choose the most effective tax strategies to achieve your goals.

Step 1: Generate Accurate Financial Statements

To develop a relevant and effective plan, as a business owner, you must know your numbers. Your financial statements need to be completed accurately because without understanding your financial performance i. e. your taxable profit for the year, any tax planning efforts are in vain.

Step 2: Understand Your Tax Position

For every taxable profit you've earned, it's important to determine your tax bracket and effective tax rate. Your tax bracket indicates the percentage of tax you'll pay on your income, while your effective tax rate reflects the average rate paid across all income.

Additionally, if you owe a balance, you should calculate your anticipated tax balance based on your projected profit for the year. Understanding these figures will help you accurately plan for your tax obligations and manage your cash flow effectively. More importantly, knowing these numbers allows you to assess whether tax planning is a necessary step for optimizing your financial situation.

Step 3: Determine Your Desired Tax Position

After gaining a clear understanding of your tax position, the most important final step in Phase I is to evaluate your satisfaction with the anticipated tax balance. For instance, if you've earned a $100K profit, how much of that are you comfortable giving to the IRS? Without any tax planning, you might owe a significant amount—possibly around $37K, depending on your tax bracket. Would you be content handing over $37K of your profit? If not, consider what steps you can take to minimize this liability. Through proper tax planning, you can explore strategies like maximizing deductions, deferring income, or income shifting, all of which can reduce your taxable income and help you avoid paying such a substantial portion of your profit to the IRS.

Phase II - Strategy Selection, Tax Allocation, and Implementation

Once your desired tax position is established, it becomes logical to explore various tax strategies, such as maximizing deductions, deferrals, and income shifting. Since each strategy comes with its own set of advantages and disadvantages, it's not advisable to rely on just one or two tax strategies.

A more effective method is to understand and consider a range of options, taking advantage of as many strategies as possible. For this reason, we recommend creating a tax strategy allocation model. This model encourages diversification, helping taxpayers avoid limiting themselves to specific tax strategies and instead embrace a broader, more balanced approach.

Step 4: Maximize Your Deductions

There are many types of deductions available for businesses, but a common misconception is that maximizing deductions always means spending money. This is simply not true. In fact, you don't always need to incur expenses to claim deductions. Sometimes, all it takes is a solid understanding of certain IRS rules and taking full advantage of them to maximize your tax savings. Whether or not these deductions require a cash outlay, the key question remains. Do you have the right system in place to capture all eligible deductions? Have you maximized every possible deduction available to you as a business owner?

Step 5: Income Shifting

Income shifting focuses on the concept of moving highly taxable income into a lower tax bracket. This can be achieved in various ways. It might involve setting up the right business entity structure to reduce your tax rate, or it could mean lowering your taxable income by employing family members, such as hiring your children to work for your business. Some key questions to consider in this step include:

i. Are you operating under the most tax-efficient entity structure?

ii. Are you missing opportunities to shift taxable income into a lower bracket?

iii. How can you implement income-shifting strategies legally without raising red flags with the IRS or triggering an audit?

Understanding and applying these strategies wisely can help reduce your overall tax burden while staying compliant with tax laws.

Step 6: Deferrals

Deferral is a common tax strategy for business owners, often associated with saving for retirement. The most common retirement vehicle is a SEP (Simplified Employee Pension) account. However, an SEP account may not be the best option for all business owners. It is essential to assess your retirement savings needs in alignment with your broader tax planning strategies. Here are some key questions business owners should consider.

   i. Do you have the right account set up for your retirement savings?
  ii. Does your current retirement plan allow you to defer a significant portion of your taxable income until retirement age?
 iii. Are there more advantageous retirement saving vehicles that could better suit your financial and tax goals?

Evaluating your retirement saving options in the context of tax planning ensures that you are maximizing both your tax benefits and long-term financial security.

Phase III - Strategy Evaluation and Final Determination

During the tax implementation phase, some business owners may face challenges when certain tax strategies become unfeasible due to cash flow constraints or other business limitations. In such situations, it's crucial for business owners to maintain open communication with their tax planners or tax accountants so that strategies can be adjusted in a timely manner. Not every strategy will suit every business owner. For instance, some deductions require detailed substantiation, and many business owners may struggle to find the time to properly document these deductions. Flexibility and ongoing dialogue are key to navigating these challenges effectively. Below, I have outlined steps that you should consider before reaching the end of the year.

Step 7: Strategy Evaluation

You may have a great tax plan, but business is ever-changing. Do you have a system in place to regularly track your progress? Any changes in your business can directly or indirectly impact your tax position. Even after implementing the tax strategies you have identified, it's just as important to update your financial statements and tax situation before year-end. By doing so, you'll be able to assess your current tax position and determine whether you have achieved your desired tax outcome. Regular reviews ensure that your tax plan remains effective and aligned with your tax goal.

Step 8: Close the Gap

With all the tax strategies you've implemented, do you have adequate supporting documentation to substantiate your deductions before claiming them on your tax return?

In this step, it's crucial to ensure that all your deductions are properly backed by records. I recommend sitting down with your tax professional to verify compliance and ensure that any risks in claiming deductions are well-calculated. This proactive approach can help you avoid potential issues with the IRS and ensure that your tax strategies taken are IRS audit-safe.

Step 9: Final Tax Balance Determination

To avoid any underpayment penalties, it is recommended that you pay most of your tax balance by the final quarterly estimated tax due date, which often falls on January 15th of the following year. To do this effectively, it is crucial to know how much you owe before the year ends. In fact, the best approach is to make quarterly estimated tax payments throughout the year. When determining your final tax balance, here are some important questions to consider.

i. What is your tax goal for the year?
ii. What was your initial anticipated tax balance?
iii. Have you made your estimated payments by the due dates?
iv. Are there any additional actions you need to take to achieve your desired tax position?

By addressing these questions, you'll ensure that you are on track to meet your tax obligations while minimizing any surprises at year-end.

Tax Planning is a Lifestyle

In the last decade, I spent a lot of time introducing businesses to the concept of **proactive tax planning**. From saving a few hundred to tens of thousands of dollars, I have witnessed many business owners benefit from these strategies. Tax planning not only helped them minimize their tax burden, but it also empowered them to make smarter decisions for their business—knowing when to spend, when to invest, and when to stop spending.

If You Want to be Proactive in Reducing Your Tax Bills, Have the Following in Mind:

1. **A proper tax plan** - Just like creating a business with clear goals and intentions, tax planning requires a well-thought-out strategy allocation model. You won't be successful if you do not have a clear tax plan with specific goals, including how much you're willing to pay to the IRS.

2. **An accurate tracking system** - Tax planning is ineffective without a proper accounting system to track and monitor all business activities. Accurate records ensure that you can take advantage of all available deductions without worrying about an IRS audit, if it happens.

Michael Gerber From The E-Myth Revisited Said This:

> "The difference between great people vs or-
> dinary people is that great people create their
> lives actively while everyone else is created by
> their lives, passively waiting to see where life
> takes them next."[3]

In many ways, tax planning operates under a similar philosophy as successful business management. If you are proactive in determining how to reduce your tax burden, you'll discover that tax planning is a powerful tool for preserving and ultimately growing your wealth.

However, if you take a reactive approach—waiting for your CPA to call or blaming your tax advisor for not providing the latest tax-saving strategies—you'll always find yourself behind the curve.

If your intention is to run a successful business, I encourage you to invest the time to read this book. By the end, I hope you'll conclude that tax planning must begin immediately if sound financial stewardship is a priority for you.

Tax planning is only meaningful if you know your numbers, understand your tax bracket, have a goal of where you want to be (how much tax you really want to pay), and how much effort you are willing to put in. Tax planning is a lifestyle!

| 2 |

WHAT ARE YOUR FINANCIAL GOALS?

Understanding your financial goals is KEY before tax planning. This is solely because tax planning should not contradict your financial goals. On the other hand, tax planning should help you achieve your financial goals. Below, I've provided a few scenarios of why you need to understand your financial goals before implementing any tax strategies.

Scenario 1: You Want to Retire Early:

If your goal is to retire early, deferring your

income should be your preferred tax strategy. Working with your CPA to maximize retirement savings may be the smartest thing to do for you.

Scenario 2: You Want to Grow Your Business Aggressively:

If your business is in a growth mode and expansion is your focus, investing in resources such as buying more equipment or spending more money in marketing your products or services may be your preferred tax strategy.

Deferral strategies such as saving for retirement would not be practical for you especially when you are trying to boost your revenue.

Scenario 3: You Want to Preserve Your Wealth:

Your business has been profitable throughout the year. In the last quarter, when you meet with your accountant, he or she advises you to increase your business expenses to offset your taxable income.

The strategy of increasing your business

expenses may not work for you if your aim is to preserve the cash you have in your business.

Often time, business owners would prefer to hold on to the cash they have in their business especially in times of uncertainties or when they are waiting to invest in some future opportunities. In this scenario, saving for retirement or investing in equipment will not work.

Scenario 4: You Plan to Sell Your Business:

If you are planning to exit your business, your financial statements from the past three years may be the key determinant of your business valuation. In this scenario, showing a good track record of consistent earnings with healthy cashflow will be important. Therefore, maximizing deductions may not work for you.

Sometimes, business owners who are planning to exit their business in the near future may prefer to minimize their write-offs in order to show a good track record of earnings.

Scenario 5: You Plan to Borrow From the Bank:

Leveraging is critical to the survival of certain businesses.

- Example: If you are in the construction business, maintaining a decent level of profitability allows you to have a good standing with your bankers.

If you are looking to borrow from financial institutions, you will need to show that your business is profitable. Hence, the route of maximizing deductions, reducing your profits to nothing, may hurt your credit rating in the long run, limiting your ability to borrow from the bank.

Conclusion

My word of advice is to always sit down with your CPA or tax professional to discuss what your financial goals are prior to considering tax planning. Effective tax planning strategies should bring you closer to your financial goals, not further away. The strategy of "Deduct, Deduct, Deduct!" may work for others, but it may not work for you.

PLANNING   37

| 3 |

WHAT IS TAX PLANNING?

Now that we have explored "Why Tax Planning" and "What Are Your Financial Goals", I presume that you would want to know what tax planning is. However, before we even begin to explore what tax planning is, let me first point out what is NOT tax planning.

Tax Planning is NOT:

Lying:

Falsifying your numbers and shortchanging the

government so that you can pay little or close to nothing.

That is not tax planning; it is tax evasion, which is a federal crime that could cost you thousands of dollars in penalties and interest, and it could even land you in prison.

Magic!

"Let's consult with an expert for an hour and learn all the tricks he or she can tell us. Afterwards, we'll pay nothing!"

Tax planning is obviously not magic. If you believe that speaking with an expert is all it takes to reduce your tax bill, then you do not truly understand the value of tax planning.

Tax Planning IS:

Compliance:

You may not believe this, but tax planning brings you a step closer to remaining in compliance with the tax authorities by legitimately deducting what they tell you to deduct.

Some business owners believe that there is not much opportunity for significant tax reductions under IRS regulations, or that existing deductions are meant to swindle taxpayers into audits. This is simply not true. Tax planning and compliance go hand in hand.

Strategy:

Remember that tax planning is not magic! Tax planning is not learning a few quick tips to reduce your tax bills. On the contrary, an effective strategy is never a quick process.

Tax planning requires detailed comparisons of different tax strategies that will benefit you. Once selected, the implementation of these strategies must be carefully monitored to ensure they are in-line with your long-term financial goals.

Tax Strategy Selection

Tax planning begins with understanding your tax situation and then selecting the right tax strategies to reduce your tax balance. These selections should not be flippantly made. For this process, you sit down with your tax professional to identify your tax strategy options after you have performed the following actions:

1. Determine Your Desired Tax Position for the Year

Based on your current income tax bracket and estimated effective tax rate, you can make a guesstimate of what you wish to pay in an ideal scenario.

- Example: If your net earnings for the year are approximately $300,000, what would your desired tax bill be in an ideal scenario based on the current trend and current tax system?

2. Complete Your Financial Goal Prioritization (FGP) Exercise

What is your financial goal? What are your main priorities? Below are a few examples. Is your goal to:

    i. Grow your business?

    ii. Retire early?

    iii. Preserve your wealth?

    iv. Invest in real estate?

    v. Achieve financial freedom and work less?

    vi. Save up for your kids' education?

The right tax plan should get you a step closer towards achieving your financial goal(s). For more details on each goal, please refer back to Chapter 2.

What Are the Right Tax Strategies for You?

Instead of learning a few tips and tricks to reduce your taxes, at XQ CPA, we believe in identifying and choosing the right tax strategies for each of our clients. There are three types of tax strategies including long-term, mid-term, and short-term strategies.

Long-Term Tax Strategies:

Long-term strategies are often more complex to understand and execute, so they require taxpayers to give some thought into them. These strategies are not impulsive, last-minute actions that can be implemented in a rush.

For example, ask yourself this: if you operate a business, do you know whether you operate under the right entity structure? Is your current entity structure benefiting you or hurting your tax position?

Another example of a long-term strategy includes setting up a retirement plan that would ensure you achieve your retirement goal within a certain timeframe.

- Scenario: You have a retirement goal of $1M, and you plan to achieve this goal in ten years. You probably will need to develop a retirement plan that allows you to at least set aside $100K per year for the next ten years.

Ideally, long-term strategies should be discussed at the beginning of every year.

Mid-Term Tax Strategies:

Mid-term strategies should be considered and discussed with your tax professional sometime around mid-year. Mid-term strategies are just as important as long-term strategies because the best time to start identifying and selecting tax strategies is after you have finalized your financial statements for the first six months of the calendar/fiscal year.

- Scenario: You have generated a taxable profit of $100K from your business during the period of January to June. By extrapolating the first six months of your monetary result, you can predict that your taxable profit for the year could potentially reach $200K or more.

From there, you will have a better understanding of how much your tax bill is going to be. Based on that understanding, you can determine what your desired tax position should be after considering various tax strategy options.

Short-Term Tax Strategies:

As the name suggests, short-term strategies are often last-minute actions that a business owner would consider due to a lack of time. These are ideal for those who did not engage in tax planning throughout the year and waited until the last thirty to sixty days before filing to reach out to their tax professional.

If a client only realizes that they are in the highest tax bracket in the last quarter of the year, some last-minute and/or immediate strategies will be most helpful in reducing their tax liability.

- Example 1: You can reduce your taxable income by prepaying certain business expenses.
- Example 2: If you are filing your taxes on a cash basis, it probably makes sense for you to delay collecting from your customers

until the following year i.e. January 1st of the following year

Developing the Right Allocation Model

By understanding your tax situation and determining your desired tax position, your tax professional should work with you to identify your long-term, mid-term, and short-term strategies. All these strategies are usually a combination of different approaches. They can include finding ways to maximize your deductions, deferring, or shifting your income to lower brackets.

Having the right allocation model is critical in tax planning because it allows you to apply and implement various tax strategies systematically throughout the year without acting hastily during tax season.

Can I Pay Nothing?

This is a common question I get almost every day. My answer is YES. If your taxable income is zero, you will pay nothing. You make zero profit in your business; you will pay nothing. What is the catch? If you run a profitable business with significant revenues but have claimed losses year after year, you may raise an IRS audit red flag.

Now let me say this, being selected for an audit does not mean you have committed a crime. If you follow the rules and can provide adequate supporting documentation, an audit is nothing more than an examination process.

Unfortunately, most of the time, many business owners do not make efforts to ensure they stay in compliance. In fact, this is the most neglected area of any business. Hence, when an IRS audit happens, most business owners panic.

How much should you really pay the IRS? What should be your desired tax position? My advice to all business owners is "Don't overpay, BUT don't underpay. PAY what you are supposed to PAY." After all, if you run a successful business, paying taxes is just part of what a profitable business needs to do.

| 4 |

UNDERSTANDING FINANCIAL
PERFORMANCE

Business owners often ask if I could teach them a few tricks to cut their tax bills significantly. *While I wish I could use a magic wand to get rid of their tax bills, tax planning is not about learning or applying JUST a few tricks.*

Proactive Tax Planning is beyond that. It is a process of mastery that empowers an individual to achieve his or her desired tax position through ongoing monitoring and application of effective tax strategies. Proactive tax planning begins when an individual realizes that he or she needs help in reducing or controlling his or her tax bills. However, from my experience, people who need tax planning may not always realize that they need it. So, the question is:

Do You Need Tax Planning?

As a business owner, you should know your **revenue, expenses, profit, and taxable income**. Let's break those down.

Revenue- Revenue represents income received from customers for the sale of goods or services performed.

- Example: If you are a shop owner, your revenue will come from the sales of your products. Meanwhile, a service provider such as a doctor or accountant will receive payments from their clients for consultation services rendered.

Expenses- Expenses represent money spent in the business, which includes rent, supplies, payroll for your employees, and more.

Profit- Profit represents the amount left over after subtracting expenses from revenue.

- Example: Say you have $80,000 in revenue and $35,000 in expenses. Your profit would then total $45,000.

Taxable income- Taxable income represents your net earnings that will be subject to taxation.

- IMPORTANT: Taxable income is different from your profit because certain deductions in your business may not be deductible when you file your taxes.

Knowing your numbers is KEY because once you have a clear understanding of your financial performance (profit or loss), it becomes easier for your CPA to "calculate" or "predict" your tax position for the tax year.

However, the challenge here is your tax position

will always fluctuate according to the profitability of your business from month to month. So, if you truly want to stay ahead in monitoring your tax position, you must have a **reliable accounting system**, a system that will allow you to **generate accurate financial statements on a monthly basis**.

Importance of Accuracy in Your Financial Statements

Financial statements- Financial statements are reports that indicate the financial performance and financial position of your business.

Income statements- More commonly known as profit and loss statements, income statements show all the contributing factors to your bottom line (net profit or loss) as mentioned above.

Revenue MINUS Expenses = PROFIT

While reviewing your financial statements,

you may find some common errors that could potentially result in missing deductions. We've highlighted a few so you know what to avoid.

Credit Cards:

For credit cards, it is important to reconcile them regularly. Failing to do so may lead to missed deductions that you are entitled to claim as expenses.

Uncashed Checks:

Checks issued to vendors or contractors that have yet to be cashed in should be considered as a deduction. Oftentimes, business owners forget to include checks issued as deductions when reporting their taxable income.

Payroll Reconciliation:

Failing to reconcile payroll correctly is another

common error made by business owners which could result in missing payroll deductions. To avoid this mistake, payroll expenses for the year need to be reconciled to all payroll reports filed with the IRS and State Workforce Commission including quarterly reports such as 941 as well as state quarterly filings and annual reports such as 940, W-2s, and W-3.

Missing Assets:

When you make a large purchase in your business, you need to be sure to record the cost of the asset at full purchase price, meaning what you have paid for.

- Example: If you buy a vehicle for your business, be sure that the cost of the car on your balance sheet is accurately reflected.

We commonly see that business owners record down payments as an expense without considering the full cost of the entire purchase. This is an area where mistakes occur often, so be sure to review your fixed assets listing against your balance sheet.

Loan Reconciliation:

If you finance a large purchase i.e., heavy equipment, it is crucial to properly reconcile your loan transactions. Failing to do so can lead to missing out on interest expense deductions.

Bad Debts:

For businesses filing on an accrual basis, it is important that you review your accounts receivable aging to make sure that any unrecoverable long outstanding debts are written off as bad debt expenses.

Conclusion

Maintaining an accurate profit and loss statement is crucial to understanding your true tax position. Beyond that, maintaining accurate financial statements is also the BEST method to protect yourself during an IRS audit.

Many business owners submit their tax returns to the IRS without understanding what they have actually reported. Some even reach the extent of allowing their tax professionals to submit their tax returns **without ever getting involved**. This could potentially increase their risk of **noncompliance**, especially if they have no idea of what is being reported to the IRS by their accountants or tax professionals.

Imagine facing an IRS Officer with a question of why your total meal expenses were $50,000 for the year, and you are clueless of how your accountant came up with the number. To avoid this, it is vital for your business to have a reliable accounting system and it is even more important that you review your financial statements – your profit and loss, and your balance sheet at least once a month, **every month**.

HOW TO GROW YOUR WEALTH THROUGH TAX PLANNING

| 5 |

CHOOSING THE RIGHT ENTITY STRUCTURE

One common area where business owners tend to neglect is operating their business with the **right entity structure**. Entity structure plays a big part in affecting your tax position. Operating under the wrong entity structure could cause business owners to **lose out on valuable deductions, overpay taxes**, or even **trigger a red flag with the IRS**, putting you at risk for an **IRS audit**.

So, what are the different entity structures, and how do you choose the right structure for your business? Below, we provide explanations on different kinds of entities.

Limited Liability Company

A Limited Liability Company, or LLC, allows you to operate your business under a separate entity from yourself. This allows asset protection of your personal assets from your business assets. As an LLC, the owner typically registers a separate Employer's Identification Number (EIN) with the IRS. The owner can then open bank accounts, enter contracts, hire employees, and obtain business licenses and permits under the EIN. Most states require annual filings and fees to remain in good standing.

Sole Proprietorship

Sole proprietors operate their business in their own name and typically report their business income and expenses on their personal tax return, under the sole proprietor's Social Security Number.

It is common for sole proprietors to register as a DBA, or Doing Business As, with the state.

Comparing LLCs and Sole Proprietorships:

Compared to a sole proprietorship, LLCs have lower risks of identity fraud since most LLCs have a separate Employer's Identification Number. It is also much easier to track your business expenses when all your business transactions occur under a dedicated bank or credit card account. This approach also increases legal protection and reduces IRS audit risks by not commingling personal funds with business funds.

Being an LLC also offers flexibility for restructuring. You may need to restructure as your business grows to reduce your tax burden. Your accountant can quickly and easily restructure your entity when you operate as an LLC. Therefore, it is a wise choice for business owners to operate their business under the proper structure from the start.

S Corporation

S corporations are popular among smaller business owners falling under these requirements:

i. Be a domestic corporation
ii. Have only allowable shareholders
   ◦ May be individuals, certain trusts, and estates and
   ◦ May not be partnerships, corporations or non-resident alien shareholders
iii. Have no more than 100 shareholders
iv. Have only one class of stock
v. Not be an ineligible corporation (i.e. certain financial institutions, insurance companies, and domestic international sales corporations).[4]

To convert an entity to become an S corporation, conversion paperwork will need to be properly filled out and submitted timely with the IRS. To operate as an S Corporation, the conversion must be approved by the IRS. This status allows corporations to pass their business income, losses, credits, and deductions to their shareholders.

Why Are S Corporations So Popular?

The reasons include S corporations help business owners avoid double taxation by allowing them to pass his or her income to an individual tax return. S corporations also enable business owners to mitigate self-employment or FICA taxes by issuing reasonable compensation and distributions. Additionally, as an S corporation, business owners do not need to pay self-employment taxes on distributions most of the time, except when distributions exceed the owner's tax basis.

However, a risk does exist for S corporations. Over the years, the IRS has found that some S corporations issue very minimal or even zero officer's compensation. The IRS sees this as an action of evading FICA taxes. If the IRS suspects a business owner of evading taxes in this manner, an IRS audit may occur.

This can result in the IRS trying to re-characterize your dividends as taxable wages. Hence, we highly recommend a reasonable compensation analysis be conducted to substantiate the amount of officer's compensation issued for the year.

Are There Any Disadvantages of Operating as an S Corporation?

Below are some key points to consider:

i. All income passed through an S corporation is taxed to shareholders, whether or not it is distributed.

ii. Additionally, shareholders who own more than 2% of the company will have some limitation on claiming certain fringe benefits as deductions.

iii. Finally, the shareholders' basis for deducting losses is increased only by direct loans to the S corporation. Other forms of funding may not allow for the deduction of losses.

   ○ Example: if your business suffers a $100K loss for the year and you have been funding your business using EIDL or SBA loans, the $100K will be suspended for tax purposes.

Should You Convert to an S Corp?

Remember that converting a business to an S corporation is often done to reduce self-employment taxes. If your business has more than $10,000 in profits, consider consulting with a tax professional to analyze the pros and cons of re-structuring your business.

C Corporation

The C corporation is an entity that is subject to double taxation. This is because C corporations are taxed separately from their owners (share-holders), resulting in corporate income taxation—currently at a rate of 21%—and individual income tax when the C corporation distributes income to individual shareholders or officers.

This creates a double taxation situation:

- First- The corporation pays taxes on its profits.
- Then- Shareholders pay taxes on dividends received.

Advantages:

Although C corporations may not be a popular

entity choice compared to S corporations, having a C corporation does come with its own advantages. C corporations do not have the same limitations as S corporations.

   i. They can have multiple classes of stock with preferences to dividends and distributions.

   ii. An unlimited number of domestic and non-US shareholders.

Basically, if you have or expect to have a large or even mega corporation that allows easy share transfer, C corporation is the way to go.

Conclusion

I get asked a lot about what entity structure should a business owner have. **It depends**. The answers vary from whether a business owner intends to keep the company as a closely held entity, or if the business owner plans to have investors down the road.

Different businesses will have unique situations, and those situations will play a key factor in the decision of what entity structure is right. Of course, making the decision to decide what entity structure is right for your business is not a light matter. If you feel that your business has reached a stage where restructuring may be beneficial, we strongly recommend that you discuss this with your tax professional before moving forward.

| 6 |

HOW AND WHAT SHOULD YOU PAY YOURSELF?

Many business owners likely do not know or do not understand that their compensation (how and what you pay yourself) has tax implications depending on the type of entity they own.

As a business owner, your goal is to **stay profitable**. If you are successful and your business is profitable, then naturally, you will want to distribute the profit for yourself in reward for all your hard work. However, in order to avoid IRS scrutiny, you must issue a **reasonable compensation**, especially if you have an S corporation.

Below, we'll discuss various types of entities and how you should pay yourself under them.

Sole Proprietorship

Compensation for sole proprietors (taxpayers filing a Schedule C) is the simplest. If you are a sole proprietor, you can issue yourself a check and call it the owner's draw.

S Corporation and C Corporation

For S and C corporations, the compensation process can be more complex. There are two methods you could go about paying yourself:

   i. Put yourself on the company's payroll.
  ii. Issue yourself a dividend distribution.

Payroll:

Putting yourself on your company's payroll comes with a major benefit: eligibility to contribute to your retirement account—if you have one.

- Example: If you have a retirement plan, such as a Simplified Employee Pension (SEP), you can contribute up to 25% of your W-2 wages.

By having a higher salary, you can contribute more to your retirement fund.

For an S corporation, you have until March 15th (or September 15th with an extension) of the following year to make your retirement contribution. This flexibility allows you to benefit from the tax deferral prior to funding your retirement by the due date.

The disadvantage to contributing to your retirement fund in this instance is that your payroll is subject to FICA (Social Security and Medicare) taxes.

As your business grows, SEP is obviously not the only retirement option you have. You could explore other retirement options such as 401(k), Simple IRA, Defined Benefit Plan, Profit Sharing Plan, and more. If your goal is to maximize retirement savings, be sure to consult with your CPA as well as a retirement specialist and/or financial advisor.

Dividend Distribution:

Alternatively, if you are a shareholder in an S corporation or C corporation, you can issue yourself a **dividend distribution**.

Unlike payroll, distributions for S corporations do not trigger FICA taxes. The catch here is that you must be extremely careful in determining your reasonable compensation. The IRS will scrutinize whether the compensation is fair based on the level of work you actively perform in the business.

- Example: If the IRS deems your compensation is unreasonably low, it might recharacterize your distributions as taxable wages.

Reasonable Compensation

How exactly do you go about determining if your compensation is reasonable? Go too high, and you end up incurring more taxes. Go too low, and the IRS may target you for an audit. So, what is deemed reasonable?

- If a business owner has a $100K profit but a W-2 wage of $50K, is that reasonable?
- Similarly, if a business owner makes a $1M profit, but draws a W-2 of $500K, is that reasonable?

As a business owner, it is important for you to understand that reasonable compensation is not solely dependent on your profitability. Instead, it is related to your distributions. All your time, effort, roles, and responsibilities contribute to how reasonable compensation should be determined. In the case of an IRS audit, you can substantiate your reasonable compensation by maintaining accurate records and following these steps:

i. **Time Tracking**- Keep a detailed log of the hours spent working on your business, along with a breakdown of the tasks you performed during those hours.

ii. **Job Description**- Create comprehensive job descriptions that outline your roles and responsibilities as a business owner. This demonstrates your value to the company.

iii. **Comparative Salary Data-** Research and gather salary data for similar positions in your industry and region to determine a reasonable compensation range.

iv. **Regular Compensation Review-** Conduct periodic reviews of your compensation structure to ensure it aligns with the business's performance and industry standards.

It may seem like a long and complicated process to determine your reasonable compensation, but by not following the proper steps and simply paying yourself what you believe is reasonable could increase your IRS audit risk.

If you are being questioned by the IRS and do not have appropriate records justifying your compensation, you could be accused of tax evasion. This could result in unnecessary tax bills with hefty penalties. Running a business is hard work, so do not let it go to waste by assuming everything is alright without taking extraordinary precautions.

Achieving the right balance between reasonable compensation and tax efficiency is key while staying in compliance with IRS regulations. If you are unsure, consult a tax professional so that you can make the right and accurate decision that will protect you and your business. With the right knowledge and guidance, you can be sure that the wages issued to yourself as an officer are in fact reasonable.

| 7 |

WHAT IS YOUR DESIRED TAX POSITION?

It was December 31st and a business owner called in a rush asking if he should purchase another large vehicle to offset his tax liability. A friend who is a business owner shared that he has been purchasing business vehicles almost every year to offset his tax bills...

It is understandable to have a strong reluctance to give your hard-earned money away to the government after working tirelessly the whole year. However, any tax strategy you have in mind should be well thought out and implemented carefully without triggering an IRS audit.

Ask any CPA if purchasing a business vehicle every year and claiming deductions for it every year is a good idea, and they will certainly tell you it sounds more like tax evasion rather than tax avoidance.

- REMEMBER: Tax avoidance is legal. Tax evasion is NOT.

What is your **Desired Tax Position**? If you run a successful business and your operation is profitable, it is inevitable that you will have to pay some taxes. After all, this is a common problem that **every** successful business owner will face.

To begin, if you have a tax problem and feel that you may be overpaying your taxes, the place to start is to **understand the size of your taxable income**. Are you going to be generating a lot more profit this year compared to the previous year, or will your income remain the same as the previous year?

Then, you need to make a guesstimate of your anticipated earnings for the year, including what will be your tax bracket, and what will be your effective tax rate. This will help you predict how high your tax bill may be and how much you will potentially have to pay the IRS.

Once you understand how much your tax bill is, then you should ask yourself what the ideal scenario would be where you will not feel that you are giving away too much of your hard-earned money. Below, I have summarized the steps that must be followed for a business owner to achieve his or her **D**esired **T**ax **P**osition.

    i. Understand your financial performance.

    ii. Understand your tax bracket and your effective tax rate.

   iii. Determine your **D**esired **T**ax **P**osition.

   iv. Identify and implement tax strategies that will get you to your **D**esired **T**ax **P**osition.

What is Your Desired Tax Position?

Steps to determine your **D**esired **T**ax **P**osition need to be exercised with reasonableness.

- Example: If you make $1M a year and you

expect to pay no tax at all, I will tell you it is not impossible; however, if you take it too far, you may end up spending all your money and will have no ability to preserve or grow your wealth.

You may be successful in paying nothing to the IRS, but your net worth will never grow. Now, if you have made a million dollars and have been paying almost 40% of taxes, then it makes sense for you to consider tax planning so that you can avoid paying 40% again.

The Secret to Avoid Paying Too Much Taxes?

In this book, we are going to share with you many ways to cut your tax bills. The main strategies to reduce your tax liability is to:

i. Maximize Deductions
ii. Maximize Deferrals
iii. Income Shifting

The reason why tax planning should start with

determining your **D**esired **T**ax **P**osition is because without establishing a tax goal, you will be implementing these strategies blindly.

- Example: If you wish to focus on increasing your deductions, you should figure out the amount of deductions you need to get to your **D**esired **T**ax **P**osition.

Similarly, if your strategy is to contribute to your retirement funds, you will need to know the amount of contributions you should make to achieve your **D**esired **T**ax **P**osition.

Regardless of how many strategies you plan to implement to achieve your **D**esired **T**ax **P**osition, one important element in tax planning is that you need CASH to optimize your tax position.

It may sound weird; you may think that a perfect candidate who needs tax planning is someone who is in a tight cashflow situation. On the contrary, a business owner who chooses to withdraw all of their funds for personal expenses is often not an ideal candidate for tax planning. In order to optimize your tax position, you need CASH.

• Example: If you plan to invest in a large machine, you may still need to make a down payment. If you wish to maximize your retirement, you need CASH to fund your retirement account. If you want to perform income shifting, i.e. shift your income to a tax shelter, you need CASH to do so.

Conclusion

Bottom line, if you run a business to fund your lifestyle and at the end of the year, have little to no savings, you will be somewhat limited in terms of the tax strategies you could implement. If you want to be tax efficient, you will need to practice responsible financial stewardship.

Always set aside at least 20% to 30% of your earnings for savings or emergency funds. Avoid spending every dollar you make. The more disciplined you are in terms of saving what you earn, the more freedom you will have to get creative when it comes to tax planning; the quicker you will be able to preserve and grow your wealth. Tax planning is not about implementing strategies blindly. It is about careful planning so that you have control over your tax position to decide how much you ultimately want to pay to the IRS.

| 8 |

WHEN AND WHAT YOU SHOULD PAY FOR ESTIMATED TAXES?

If you run a business and it has been generating profit, you should pay estimated taxes on a quarterly basis to avoid any underpayment penalties. Estimated tax payment dates are as follows:

- January 1 to March 31 - **April 15**
- April 1 to May 31 - **June 15**
- June 1 to August 31 - **September 15**
- September 1 to December 31 - **January 15 of the following year**

What Are Estimated Taxes?

Estimated tax payments are quarterly payments made based on your earnings for the period. Essentially, estimated tax allows you to prepay a portion of your income tax once in every few months to avoid paying a lump sum when your tax return is due. If you expect to owe tax of $1000 or more when you file your tax return, the IRS expects you to make estimated tax payments. Quarterly tax payments are generally applicable to self-employed individuals and business owners.

How Do You Calculate Quarterly Estimated Taxes?

There are a few ways to calculate your quarterly tax payments depending on the nature of your business and its earnings cycle.

If you earn a steady and recurring income, calculate or project the tax you'll owe for the year and send 25% to the IRS each quarter. You need to include FICA taxes if you are a sole proprietor or a single-member LLC filing as a disregarded entity.

If your income is seasonal and your earnings fluctuate throughout the year, you can estimate your tax burden based on your income and deductions in the previous quarter.

If you have not been making adequate estimated payments, you may incur an underpayment penalty when you file your 1040 (personal tax return). Generally, individuals must pay the lesser of 100% of last year's tax or 90% of this year's tax to avoid an underpayment penalty. However, this rule changes if you earn more than $150K. In that case, you must pay the lesser of 110% of last year's tax or 90% of this year's tax if your adjusted gross income (AGI) for the last year exceeded $150K.

Do I Have to Pay Estimated Taxes as a W-2?

If you earn or receive income that is not subject to federal withholding taxes, such as side hustle earnings, you'll pay as you go with estimated taxes. If you expect to receive some other income such as investment income (i.e. dividends, interests, capital gain), royalties, employment benefits, social security benefits, prizes/awards, you may need to also consider making estimated payments.

How Do I Pay My 1040-ES?

You may send estimated tax payments via Form 1040-ES. Better yet, you can pay online, by phone, or from your mobile device using the IRS2Go app. Visit IRS.gov/payments to view all the options.

Should You Be Paying Estimated Taxes?

You should be making estimated payments if you are the kind of business owner who:

i. Doesn't like to pay any penalties and would avoid them at all costs.
ii. Doesn't want to accumulate a large tax bill when it comes to tax time.
iii. Has somewhat of a predictable income stream throughout the year and wants to have better control of your cashflow position.

Why Do Some Business Owners Prefer to Pay by April 15?

Although we recommend all business owners to make regular estimated payments on a quarterly basis, some business owners prefer not to do so due to the following reasons:

i. Business owners need cash to operate their business. In some cases, income is unstable, so keeping cash may be vital to survive. This is especially true for those in the construction business.

ii. Business owners may have better investment opportunities that would bring a higher return, so they prefer to invest the cash rather than giving it to the IRS.

iii. Business owners don't mind paying penalties.

Conclusion

When it comes to making estimated payments, I am a firm believer that responsible business owners should comply. I believe that doing the right thing will get you where you need to be.

From my years of running my own practice dealing with business owners, I have served many business owners. Those who are successful in their business tend to want to follow the rules and do the right thing.

It is also my firm belief that you should not keep what does not ultimately belong to you. Making regular estimated payments allows you to plan better by truly understanding your cashflow position. It encourages better financial steward-ship and helps avoid unnecessary surprises, that in turn allow you to focus and grow your business.

| 9 |

SETTING UP YOUR
RETIREMENT PLAN

Now that you've learned about the importance of having the right entity structure and how you should pay yourself, the next important subject is retirement planning.

Many business owners tend to put off this subject because they think that if the business is profitable, they do not need to worry about retirement planning. Many fail to realize that planning for retirement is important. There are many tax benefits associated with proper retirement planning, so in this chapter, we will introduce you to various retirement plan options and how to make the most of them to optimize your tax position.

Tax Benefit:

The main reason why retirement savings could lower your taxes is because retirement contributions defer your tax obligations until later in life.

Types of Retirement Plans

There are many retirements plans to choose from: Solo 401(k), 401(k) and Profit Sharing, Simple IRA, SEP IRA, self-directed IRA, defined benefit plan, and more.

Simplified Employee Pension (SEP) IRA:

The Simplified Employee Pension (SEP) IRA is a popular choice for many business owners due to its ease of setup and low operating costs.

This plan allows employers to contribute to their own retirement accounts at higher levels than traditional IRAs, making it desirable to small business owners and self-employed individuals. Additionally, SEP IRAs provide flexibility in timing of contributions.

- Example: In the year 2023, you can decide to contribute to SEP IRA but do not need to fund your retirement account until your tax filing due date of your business tax return i.e. March 15th or September 15th if you have filed an extension for an S corporation.

How do you contribute to an SEP IRA account?

i. Sole Proprietor: personal funds
ii. S Corporation: business funds

With its low cost of commitment and tax-deferral benefits, the SEP IRA is a smart choice for retirement saving, especially for startups. Without huge cash commitments, this plan allows you to focus on the growth and expansion of your business.

Solo 401(k):

The Solo 401(k) is a compelling option for those who own 100% of their business and do not have employees.

It gives you the ability to maximize your retirement contribution without maximizing your W-2 wages.

- Example: If you have an SEP plan, for a $100K W-2, you will be limited to contribution amount of $25,000. However, if you have a Solo 401(k), for a $50K W-2, you are able to maximize your contribution up to $35,000, or more depending on the 401(k) contribution limit approved by the IRS for that particular year.

This is because for Solo 401(k) plan, the business owner is able to contribute to both the employee and employer portion of the 401(k) plan, allowing the owner to maximize their contribution compared to the SEP plan.

If you are looking to aggressively increase your retirement savings so that you can accumulate retirement funds quicker, adding profit sharing plan and/or defined benefit plan in addition to your 401(k) is another method.

Defined Benefit Plan:

A defined benefit plan is an employer-sponsored retirement plan that calculates employee benefits based on factors such as salary history and length of employment.

This plan allows employees to receive a predetermined amount of retirement income, which provides more financial security during retirement. Instead of employees being responsible for investment risk, in a defined benefit plan, the employer takes on all the planning and investment risks. This makes it a valuable option for those wanting a reliable retirement income stream.

A defined benefit plan is usually suitable for established businesses with steady cashflow.

Simple IRA:

Simple IRA is a great option for business owners who want to make retirement contributions for both them and their employees but would like to avoid costly administrative fees associated with a traditional 401(k) plan.

The Simple IRA allows both the employer and the employee to make contributions, with varying matching options available.

Self-Directed IRA:

If you have a desire to invest in assets beyond the scope of traditional retirement accounts, a self-directed IRA could be the right choice for you. Many might dream of investing in real estate using their retirement account; with a self-directed IRA, this is possible.

What exactly is a self-directed IRA? A self-directed IRA is a unique type of individual retirement account that offers the flexibility to invest in assets not typically allowed by conventional retirement accounts.

A word of caution for those who are looking into setting up self-directed retirement accounts. Please exercise caution and adhere to the rules to avoid engaging in prohibited transactions such as life insurance and collectibles.

This is critical to consider when choosing

an unconventional retirement plan. Any presence of prohibited transactions or assets in your self-directed IRA can lead to its dissolution, leaving you responsible for all taxes, fees, and penalties. To avoid any surprises, it is vital to consult with your tax professional before venturing into this plan.

Conclusion

When selecting a retirement plan, consider various factors, including contribution limits, administrative costs, and your financial goals in the long run. Make sure to come to a decision and set up your account timely so that you can maximize your tax benefits and begin funding your retirement account sooner than later.

Hopefully now you gain a better understanding of the importance of choosing the right retirement plan for yourself and your employees. With this knowledge, you are now one step closer to maximizing tax savings through deferral strategies.

| 10 |

MAXIMIZING HOME OFFICE
DEDUCTIONS

Now that you have an overview of what is tax planning, entity structure, and tax deferral strategies, another important aspect of tax planning is to make sure you maximize your tax deductions.

Many business owners lose out on important tax deductions because they either do not track their deductions, or they simply don't know that they are able to claim them. One of the most commonly missed deductions is the **home office deduction**.

Some of you may have heard that if you claim

home office deductions, you could potentially trigger an **IRS audit**. This is simply **not true**. In fact, the IRS actually wants you to claim your home office deduction, so much so that since 2013, the IRS began offering a simplified option to make it easier for more taxpayers to claim the deduction.

Simplified Method:

This method uses a prescribed rate of $5 per square foot multiplied by the allowable square footage used in the home. However, if your intent is to maximize your home office deductions, then we recommend you use the Regular Method, which we will explain further.

What is the Home Office Deduction?

The home office deduction is a deduction that the IRS allows for self-employed individuals who work from home.

To determine whether you are eligible to claim the home office deduction, refer to the checklist below:

i. W-2 employees are not eligible to claim the home office deduction.

ii. The home office deduction, calculated on Form 8829, is available to both homeowners and renters.

iii. There are certain expenses taxpayers can deduct. These may include mortgage interest, insurance, utilities, repairs, maintenance, depreciation, and rent.

iv. Taxpayers must meet specific requirements to claim home expenses as a deduction. Even then, the deductible amount of these expenses may be limited.

v. The term "home" for purposes of this deduction:

   ○ Includes a house, apartment, condominium, mobile home, boat, or similar property.

   ○ Also includes structures on the property. These are places like an unattached garage, studio, barn, or greenhouse.

   ○ Does not include any part of the taxpayer's property used exclusively as a hotel, motel, inn, or a similar business.

vi. Generally, there are two basic requirements for the taxpayer's home to qualify as a deduction.

1. There must be exclusive use of a portion of the home for conducting business on a regular basis.

   - Example: a taxpayer who uses an extra room to run their business can take a home office deduction only for that extra room so long as it is used both **regularly** and **exclusively** for the business.

2. The home must generally be the taxpayer's principal place of business. A taxpayer can also meet this requirement if administrative or management activities are conducted at the home and there is no other location to perform those duties.

   - Therefore, **someone who conducts business outside of**

their home but also uses their home to conduct business may still qualify for a home office deduction.

vii. Expenses that relate to a separate structure not attached to the home may qualify for a home office deduction. They will only qualify if the structure is used exclusively and regularly for business.

viii. Taxpayers who qualify may choose one of two methods to calculate their home office deduction:

1. **Simplified Method:** Has a rate of $5 per square foot for business use of the home. The maximum size for this option is 300 square feet, meaning that the maximum deduction under this method is $1,500.

2. **Regular Method:** Deductions for a home office are based on the percentage of the home devoted to business use. Taxpayers who use a whole room or part of a room for their business need to figure out the percentage of

the home used for business activities to deduct indirect expenses.

- Direct expenses are deducted in full.

How to Claim Home Office Expenses

If you are a sole proprietor filing a Sch C, you can take the deduction directly on the Schedule C using the Simplified Method. Alternatively, if you wish to maximize home office deductions, we recommend you fill out Form 8829 and submit along with your Sch C to use the Regular Method.

Conclusion

To sum up, if you do not want to give your hard-earned money away, every single deduction counts. Oftentimes, business owners feel that it's a waste of time to track all these deductions. What they do not realize is that these missing deductions could ultimately have an effect on what tax bracket they will be in. This then affects your effective tax rate and the tax bills you will have to pay at the end of the day, so do not give away this deduction that can save you hundreds—if not thousands—of dollars.

If you are still skeptical about claiming home office deductions after reading this chapter, we strongly recommend that you consult with a CPA or a Tax Planner who can provide you with further guidance on claiming this deduction.

| 11 |

MAXIMIZING AUTO DEDUCTIONS

Just like home office deductions, **auto deductions** are also commonly missed by many business owners, especially for those who do not track their business mileage. For business owners and independent contractors who drive regularly to meet existing and prospective clients, claiming auto deductions is a no brainer, but in order to make the most out of them, you need to understand how they work.

First of all, do you have a **business vehicle**? This can be a car you already own or lease and have converted to business use, or a car you bought or leased for the exclusive purpose of business use.

Purchasing VS Leasing

A question many business owners ask is if they should buy a vehicle or lease. Unfortunately, the answer is not very straightforward, as there are advantages and disadvantages to both options.

Purchasing a Business Vehicle:

The most appealing reason to purchase a business vehicle under your business name is that it allows you to maximize your deductions by claiming S179, or bonus depreciation.

- Example: If you buy an SUV exceeding 6,000 lb. worth $100K, in 2023, you are allowed to maximize your depreciation up to 80% of the purchase cost, provided you can substantiate your **Business Use Percentage (BUP)** by maintaining a mileage log.

The downside of maximizing auto depreciation is that once you take the full deduction in the first year of purchase, you are required to keep the vehicle above a Business Use Percentage of 50% for the next five years. If you dispose the business vehicle within those five years, the bonus depreciation claimed will be recaptured as income.

Leasing a Business Vehicle:

When leasing a business vehicle, you can deduct the BUP of the vehicle's monthly payment. Combined with a generally lower upfront payment and the excitement of driving a brand-new vehicle every few years, leasing can sound more appealing to some business owners.

On the downside, you will not have a significant depreciation bonus to claim, and dealerships typically insert a yearly mileage limit in your lease contract.

As you have likely started to realize, auto deductions are not as simple as they appear, but understanding the distinction between how you could claim deductions under both options should allow you to come to a decision on whether you should buy or lease a business vehicle.

Choosing the Best Auto Deduction Method

So, now that you have a car that is ready to be put to work, you must decide which auto deduction method is best for your tax position.

Standard Method:

The first method is called the **Standard Method**, also known as the **Standard Mileage Rate** or the **Mileage Method**. It involves a standardized deduction rate for business miles driven that the IRS sets for every tax year.

The advantage to this method is its simplicity for taxpayers who do not wish to keep all their actual receipts for repairs, car washes, car insurance, etc. Rather, the only record you must keep is an accurate mileage log.

What is Considered a Business Mile?

Any trip related to business is considered a business mile. When you track miles driven for business purposes, the starting point must be your principal place of business. In other words, you can start your trip from your office and then drive to your clients' office or worksite.

- IMPORTANT: The commute from your home to your principal place of business does not count unless you have a **home office**.

What if you operate from both your home office as well as a separate business premises where you meet with your business contacts? In that instance, you are allowed to claim your business trip from your home office provided you use your home office regularly and exclusively as part of your business operation.

- Example: You take a day trip to your client's office to negotiate a deal, and the distance between your office and the client's office is

55 miles. The round-trip totals 110 miles, and the standard rate for 2023 is 65.5 cents per mile. This means that the trip to your client's office and back will earn you 7,205 cents, or $72.05.

If after a year of using the Standard Mileage Rate, you do not feel like you are getting the maximum benefits, you can elect to switch to the **Actual Expense Method**, as long as you started using the Standard Mileage Method in the first year after you placed your business vehicle in service.

- IMPORTANT: It is crucial to note that you cannot use the Standard Mileage Rate if you own five or more cars simultaneously, which would be considered a fleet operation.

Actual Method:

How does the Actual Expenses Method work? Rather than keeping just a mileage log, the Actual Expenses Method involves meticulous and careful record-keeping of all expenses related to your business vehicle. This includes receipts for your gas, car insurance, lease payments, car washes, maintenance, repairs, licenses, vehicle registrations, and any other expenses associated with your vehicle.

It can be tedious for some business owners, and if you lose any of your records—especially huge repair bills—you may have difficulty substantiating your deductions during an IRS audit. However, this should not discourage you from choosing the Actual Expenses Method. If you charge all your business vehicle expenses to your business credit card, tracking your auto deductions should be a lot easier. Just remember that you should be in the habit of staying organized and mindful of notating all of your business trips and related vehicle expenses.

Switching Between Standard Method and Actual Method

If you want to use the Standard Mileage Rate to calculate vehicle expenses, you must choose it in the **first year you use the car for business**.

In later years, you can use the Standard Mileage Rate or switch to the Actual Expenses Method.

If you use Actual Expenses for the vehicle (even if it's the first year you used it for business), **you cannot switch to the Standard Mileage Rate.** As long as you use that car for business, you **must** continue to use the Actual Method. Hence, claiming the Section 179 deduction or bonus depreciation will make you ineligible for the Standard Method.

Conclusion

As you can see, both methods have their advantages and disadvantages, and which method you choose depends on how much of the deduction you will enjoy from the method you use. Regardless of which method you choose, it is imperative you maintain sufficient records to substantiate your deductions, especially maintaining a mileage log to prove your Business Use Percentage.

If you use the Standard Mileage Rate, you must have records of business versus personal miles driven. If you use the Actual Expenses Method, you must have records of all expenses, and you must allocate them between business and personal use. **Tolls and parking fees are always deductible, no matter which deduction method you use.**

If you are planning to invest in a business vehicle and are not sure of which method would help you maximize your tax benefits, we recommend that you consult with a tax professional to conduct a more in-depth analysis based on your specific situation.

| 12 |

RE-INVESTING FOR
LONG-TERM GROWTH

In this chapter, we are going to share with you how you could leverage tax planning for long-term growth by investing in **revenue-generating assets**.

The word "assets" can be broad. In the world of tax planning, we often refer to tangible assets such as equipment and machinery that can boost the productivity of your operation.

Investing in assets that are essential for your business not only helps increase your revenue generation capacity, but they could also provide huge tax savings for yourself or your business.

- Example: When you purchase a machine worth $100K, your vendor may only require a 10% down payment if you finance the rest of the cost. However, if you place the machine in service before December 31st, you may claim a depreciation deduction up to 80% of the full cost of your equipment, in the scenario that bonus depreciation is allowed.

This strategy not only helps you preserve cash, but it also helps you boost your profitability, and at the same time, minimize your tax liability.

What is Depreciation?

In case you need a refresher, **depreciation is the reduction in the value of an asset over time due to wear and tear or obsolescence**. Fortunately, the IRS allows businesses to recover the cost of qualifying equipment and machinery through depreciation deductions.

Sounds Great Right?

What else may you need to watch out for? While deciding to make a huge purchase, we do recommend working with a tax professional or CPA to guide you when you plan to maximize your deduction through S179 or bonus depreciation. This is due to other factors you will need to consider.

- Example: If you own an S corporation, you will need to have sufficient basis as a shareholder to enjoy the deduction.

Basis- The amount of investment a taxpayer has in a business.

- IMPORTANT: Keep track of basis year over year because it can hinder the shareholder's ability to use losses that pass through from an S corporation.

Conclusion

Investing in revenue-generating assets can be a great strategy for many businesses, as it not only brings benefits to the business, it also provides substantial tax savings that could reduce tax bills. If you feel that this strategy is right for your business, you should consider this strategy as part of your tax plan.

| 13 |

HIRING YOUR KIDS

The next strategy we want to discuss with you is powerful because it allows you to shift your income to the **zero tax bracket**. That's right, zero! And the best part is it's entirely by the book and legal! The strategy? **Hire your kids to work for you**.

For many small businesses, family members often step in whenever they need extra help. If your children are regularly assisting you in your business, why not consider offering them an employment contract? The pay doesn't have to be excessive; it just needs to be reasonable for their time and effort put into your business.

The Advantage:

If your child is not receiving a huge salary, they may end up in the zero tax bracket. This means that **the first $13,850 you pay your child, or up to the standard deduction limit for the year, could technically be tax-free.**

How?

The standard deduction for single filers in 2023 is $13,850. Assuming that you pay your child the federal minimum wage at $7.25/hour, then your child's full-time annual income will be $15,080. After taking the standard deduction, they will be left with just $1,230 in taxable income.

If your child only works part time and earns less than $13,850 per year, then they technically could use their standard deduction to offset their entire income, resulting in no taxable income at all.

- IMPORTANT: If you have more than one child working for your business, you can potentially shift double or even triple the income i.e. two kids for $27,700, and three for $41,550.

What's the Catch?

You might think this strategy sounds too good to be true. The catch here is that you must hire your kids to do real work. In addition, **the FLSA sets minimum age for employment at 14 years old**, and it limits the number of hours worked by minors under the age of 16.

To prove the legitimacy of your kid's employment, you should treat them as you would a regular employee. That means taking the following steps:

i. Draw up a proper employment contract with terms and conditions.
ii. Provide a job description detailing their roles and responsibilities.
iii. Keep accurate timesheets of their daily tasks performed.
iv. Make sure the salary rate is fair based on the time and difficulty of the work performed.

Important:

Make sure you stay in compliance with the IRS while implementing the strategy of hiring your children.

- Example: If you operate an S or C corporation, you will have to pay FICA (Social Security and Medicare) taxes.
- Meanwhile: If you operate your business as a disregarded entity i.e. a single member LLC or sole proprietorship, your child's salary is exempt from Social Security, Medicare, and FUTA taxes if certain conditions are met.
  - Your child must be under the age of 18 for this to apply (or under 21 in the case of the FUTA tax exemption).

Conclusion

While it is great to benefit from the zero tax bracket by passing your income to your kids, hiring them to work for you has advantages beyond taxes. It is an excellent way for your kids to develop real life skills and build a strong work ethic.

So, if your kids intend to help you in your business, or they are already doing some work for you, maybe it is time for you to start recruiting them.

| 14 |

HOW TO SHIFT YOUR PERSONAL INCOME TO A CORPORATION

In previous chapters, we discussed several tax strategies, including how to maximize deductions and how to utilize retirement contributions to defer your taxable income. If you are a serial entrepreneur who owns several businesses, this next strategy will bring tremendous tax savings, and at the same time, help you preserve more cash for you to grow your business.

This strategy involves shifting your taxable income to a corporation by setting up a

Management Service Organization for your other businesses.

What is a Management Service Organization?

A Management Service Organization (MSO) is an entity that provides business services to an **Operating Company (OC),** or multiple Operating Companies, whichever is applicable. These business services include, but are not limited to:

  i. Human Resources (HR)
 ii. Staffing
iii. Information Technology (IT)
 iv. Accounting
  v. Marketing
 vi. Sales
vii. Other Administrative Services

There are some industries (e.g. healthcare) that use this approach extensively. The reality is that this structure can be utilized by just about any industry.

Examples of MSO Services to an Operating Company

Operational Issues:

i. Handle all marketing and public relations for the Operating Company.

ii. Assist the Operating Company in developing business plans.

iii. Maintain and update all policies and procedures for the Operating Company.

iv. Handle phone or written inquiries regarding the Operating Company's services or goods.

v. Disaster Recovery and/or Business Continuity Plan.

Financial Management:

i. Deposit checks and maintain banking records.

ii. Assist with management of the Operating Company's budget.

iii. Provide accounting and bookkeeping services.

Human Resources and Personnel Management:

i. Hiring, on-boarding, training, and developing personnel.

ii. Support the Operating Company in obtaining insurance, benefits, and related coverages.

iii. Provide any other HR-related functions for the Operating Company.

Staff Education and Training:

i. Hire and train staff who support the services offered by the Operating Company.

Tax Savings When Using an MSO

When structured properly, MSOs can offer numerous tax advantages and tax planning strategies not available in the traditional "passed-through" environment of most Operating Companies.

These efficiencies stem from the MSO being structured as a C corporation, which is taxed at a flat rate of 21% on all income. An MSO can also have a fiscal year-end that works in conjunction with the calendar year-end of your Operating Company. The fiscal year allows for the deferral of income recognition as well as more time for tax planning efficiencies and opportunities.

There are many benefits associated with this course of action. Let's explore them.

Lower Tax Rate:

A significant advantage of a C corporation is its lower tax rate. For high-net-worth individuals facing a tax rate of 37% or higher, the shift to a corporation with a lower tax rate (21%) will immediately create greater tax savings for business owners.

Mitigating Double Taxation:

While most people typically think that C corporations face double taxation, there are strategies to mitigate this. Maximizing salaries or optimizing compensation in specific years can help you avoid the double tax situation.

Dividend Tax Deferral:

Unlike S corporations where you are taxed on profits regardless of withdrawals, C corporations allow you to defer dividend tax until you choose to withdraw the money. This can be a powerful financial planning tool.

Fringe Benefits:

Another key advantage lies in fringe benefits. In a C corporation, group health insurance and education assistance—when extended to all employees, including officers, are deductible.

Downside

The downside to an MSO is that managing a C corporation is not as simple as an LLC. There are additional compliance regulations you must follow.

- Example: A proper management contract between the MSO and your Operating Company needs to be in place to substantiate the type of services your MSO will provide to your Operating Company.

- ○ Your Operating Company will need to pay a **Management Fee** equal to the fair market value of those services. The fair market value is calculated with a **Management Fee Analysis (MFA)**.

Management Fee Analysis:

The MFA is based upon services rendered, the amount of time, experience, and proficiency of the service provider for businesses within your operating area and industry segment. This information is based on 3rd party data from the US government as well as industry studies.

Since you own both the Operating Company and the MSO, payments between these entities will be deemed to be related party transactions. As such, we must follow the guidelines of what constitutes reasonable compensation and appropriate transfer pricing for those services.

Once the Management Fee Analysis has been

completed and the MSA signed, your MSO can begin providing services to the Operating Company, and the Operating Company can then pay the MSO for those services.

Conclusion

Some entrepreneurs managing multiple businesses find it in their best interest to establish a management company to provide services to its operating units. This decision is not one to be taken lightly, so it would be in your favor to consult with your CPA if you intend to set up an MSO for your business.

Compared to the strategies we discussed in earlier chapters, it is certain that the MSO strategy is a more complex one. If you are not sure about executing this strategy, we encourage you to reach out to our experts at XQ CPA for guidance.

| 15 |

TAKING ADVANTAGE OF
SAFE HARBOR RULES

Imagine that the end of the year is approaching, and you suddenly realize that your tax balance will be quite high for the year due to higher profits your business has generated throughout the year. What's the best last-minute tax strategy that will lower your tax bill in this situation? The **safe harbor** rule.

An effective way to execute this strategy is to consider all the expenses that you will incur for the next 12 months and either prepaying them through your business credit card or by check.

This way, you can enjoy the deduction now and not have to wait until the following year. This is because you can deduct those expenses paid in the current year, enabling you to offset your expenses against your taxable income now rather than later.

- Example: The year is 2023, and your office rent is $3K every month. Before the start of 2024, you can prepay rent for January, February, and March, totaling $9K. Since you paid before the new year, you can deduct those $9K of rent when filing your 2023 tax return.

Below are some examples of deductions you could prepay to take advantage of the safe harbor rule:

Advertising	Education	Legal Fees
Accounting	Employee Benefits	Software Expenses
Business License	Training	Office Supplies

Books	Furniture	Tools
Bonuses	Business Travel	Client Gifts
Computers	Business Meetings	Holiday Gatherings
Conferences	Business Insurance	Rent Expenses
Dues and Subscriptions	Uniforms	Utilities
Office Décor	Software Renewals	Repairs
Display	Marketing	Contract Labor
Employee Gifts	Coaching	Janitorial

How to Implement

There are two ways to implement this strategy:

1. Charge expenses to your business credit card.
   - This will serve as evidence for transactions incurred.

2. Issue a check to the vendor or contractor.
    ◦ You need to make sure that the check is dated correctly i.e. by or before December 31st if your tax filing year aligns with the calendar year.

To implement the safe harbor rule correctly, you will need to create a list of all possible expenses you plan to or may incur in the following year. We recommend that you review your income statements (also known as profit and loss statements) to identify the type of recurring expenses that are necessary and likely to occur in the next quarter or year.

Then, assess your cashflow situation to determine your ability to make prepayments. If your cashflow is low, then the only way for you to implement this strategy is to charge these expenses to your business credit card.

This process takes time if you want to execute it correctly. Paying for something you do not need could result in wastages. You may need outside assistance to conduct detailed analysis, so do not hesitate to reach out to a CPA or tax professional for guidance!

Now, like all tax strategies, you will need to keep detailed documentation of your spending. That is why we recommend using business credit cards or checks so that there will always be a paper trail to follow in the case of an IRS audit. Even if the IRS does not audit you, it is always a good practice to maintain adequate supporting documentation to avoid potential issues in the future.

Conclusion

As a business owner, working hard all year long just to give away your hard-earned money to the IRS is a waste of time. Our goal is to arm you with the right strategies to become more tax efficient. If implemented correctly, the safe harbor rule can be a fantastic way to reduce your taxable income just before the end of the year.

| 16 |

HOW TO STAY OUT OF
TROUBLE FROM THE IRS

Some business owners interpret tax planning as "getting creative" and being less "by the book". As a CPA and Certified Tax Coach, I want to emphasize that **tax planning is in no way asking you to evade taxes**. On the contrary, I believe that business owners who carry out proper tax planning tend to stay in compliance so that they stay out of trouble from the IRS. **Tax planning is not tax evasion**. It is tax avoidance, which is legal! Evasion is **not**.

As we enter the final chapter of this book, I

want to share with you a few tips to stay under the
IRS radar and avoid an IRS audit. These tips will
enable you to avoid some common errors made by
others, keeping you **safe** with the IRS.

Avoid the Zeros:

Filing your taxes based on estimates or round-
ing numbers is an unwise practice. Estimates are
not accurate and could raise red flags with the
IRS. It is essential to have proper documentation
and accurate records for all deductions claimed.
Instead of guessing, take the time to track and
record your actual expenses diligently.

Lack of Proof or Substantiation:

Claiming deductions without proper documentation is not just risky; it could be dangerous.
If you cannot provide evidence to support your
deduction, it is better to not even claim it on your
tax return.

- Example: Let's say you want to claim miles
  driven for business purposes on your tax

return, and you did not maintain an accurate mileage log. Simply guessing without adequate substantiation could result in the IRS disregarding your deduction, ultimately costing you additional taxes, interests, and penalties.

This does not just apply to auto deductions. Hence, making sure you maintain detailed and sufficient supporting documentation for all business deductions throughout the year is important.

Errors on Financial Statements:

Some business owners assume that QuickBooks can do wonders. The reality is that though the Bank Feed feature allows you to import transactions directly from your bank, it does not mean that QuickBooks can reconcile your books or code transactions correctly for you. Just because your transactions have been imported does not mean that your financial statements are accurate.

Oftentimes, we see transactions being duplicated or missed, resulting in an over/understatement of income and/or expenses, which could be

detrimental to your tax position. Failure to reconcile your books accurately can result in inaccurate
financial statements and tax filings.

Other Common Errors:

A common set of errors people tend to over-
look are clerical errors. These can include missing
or inaccurate Social Security Numbers. Electronic
filing will detect SSN errors instantly. Paper filing
may lead to delays in detecting and correcting
these kinds of mistakes.

Additionally, we see that names are often mis-
spelled. Double check for any typos before you
send in your tax return. Remember, the spelling
must match what is shown on the Social Security
card. If you do not have an SSN, be certain that
your Individual Tax Identification Number (ITIN)
is not expired.

If you opt for direct deposit, you need to
check your bank details. If your account or rout-
ing numbers are incorrect, your tax refund could
be delayed.

You need to be sure you use the correct filing
status. If you are married, file as a married couple.

Unmarried individuals should file accordingly. Not doing so can lead to errors in tax calculations.

Mathematical errors are also common, so we recommend investing in a proper accounting system to compile financial statements.

Some business owners commingle their business funds with personal expenses. Mixing the two (personal and business) can lead to confusion and potential mistakes. A good way to avoid this is to maintain separate accounts for personal and business expenses.

Below, we've provided a checklist of what business owners need to watch out for while submitting their tax returns to the IRS:

i. All bank statements recorded and reconciled on a monthly basis.
ii. All credit card statements recorded and reconciled on a monthly basis.
iii. All loan statements recorded and reconciled on a monthly basis.
iv. All payroll and payroll taxes recorded and reconciled to the payroll reports filed with the IRS and local taxing authority.

v. All out-of-pocket expenses properly recorded.

vi. All retirement contributions funded in a timely manner.

vii. All home office deductions reimbursed timely and accurately.

viii. All mileage logs completed with proper substantiation.

ix. All client meals/meeting logs properly documented.

x. Receipts properly scanned for all meals above $75.

Conclusion

To minimize errors, business owners should at least avoid paper filing. Electronic filing is more efficient and reduces the risk of your tax return being lost in the mail or your refund being delayed due to delayed processing. In addition, business owners should avoid manual calculations. We recommend using proper accounting systems like QuickBooks or Xero rather than Excel to record your income and expenses.

Avoiding these common errors is essential for any business owner looking to optimize their tax position. By maintaining accurate records and seeking professional guidance, you can ensure that you monitor your tax position to minimize any unwanted surprises. Remember that tax planning is an ongoing process, and regular review of your financial performance and tax situation is key to maximizing your tax savings.

CONCLUSION

Is tax planning **beneficial**? Is tax planning **real**? When tax planning was first introduced to me, I was made to believe that some practitioners would charge their clients tens of thousands of dollars for just selling a book filled with tax strategies. Since then, I have met business owners who told me they no longer believe in tax planning because they got nothing out of it.

I think the issue here is that many business owners do not realize that successful tax planning does not ultimately rely on *who* you hire as a tax planner. Rather, it relies on *how* you implement the tax strategies that your tax planner has given you.

Tax planning begins with identifying the right strategies for you and your business, but without implementing them fully, tax savings can never be materialized.

Below, I summarize the process of tax planning and the percentage of time you should spend or dedicate for each segment:

- Strategy Selection – **10%**
- Tax Allocation – **10%**
- Strategy Implementation – **60%**
- Final Determination – **20%**

If you are a business owner who has finished reading the 16 chapters of this book, I want to congratulate you! If you are willing to put in the time to gain extra knowledge on how to better "tax plan", it means you are a responsible business owner who takes financial stewardship seriously. You don't want to overpay in taxes, but you also don't want to shortchange the government. You want to pay what is JUST RIGHT for yourself, your business, and for the IRS.

In closing, it is my wish that business owners will truly understand the REAL meaning of tax planning and WHY it is critical in accelerating your wealth building. If you want to tax plan successfully, please remember that tax planning is beyond just learning a few tricks.

"Tax planning is a lifestyle that will empower businesses to make better decisions through practicing better financial stewardship..."

BIBLIOGRAPHY

1. Main, Kelly. "Small Business Statistics of 2024." Forbes, Forbes Magazine, 14 Nov. 2023, www.forbes.com/advisor/business/small-business-statistics/.

2. IRS. "Worksheet Solutions The Difference Between Tax Avoidance and Tax Evasion." https://apps.irs.gov/app/understandingTaxes/whys/thm01/les03/media/ws_ans_thm01_les03.pdf

3. Gerber, Michael E. *The E-Myth Revisited*. VisAbility Ltd, 2021.

4. "S Corporations." *Internal Revenue Service*, www.irs.gov/businesses/small-businesses-self-employed/s-corporations.

AUTHOR'S NOTE

When I was first introduced to the concept of tax planning, I was told it was one of the fastest paths to maximizing returns in a practice. I was shown a system that allowed tax practitioners to instantly print pages of tax strategies to present to clients. We were then taught to price each tax plan at 30% to 50% of the actual tax savings. Tax planning service, as presented by many professionals, was heavily focused on benefiting the tax practitioners rather than truly serving the everyday business owner.

The truth is, no matter how much tax savings a client realizes, I could never bring myself to charge such a high fee. I don't believe in running a tax planning business with a churn-and-burn mentality. To me, tax planning is an essential process for every business, as effective tax planning ultimately helps businesses grow stronger and wealthier.

To Montserrat, my dedicated team member, thank you for your time and commitment in recording every video with me, transcribing them chapter by chapter, and editing and re-editing them repeatedly and patiently. I couldn't have accomplished this without your unwavering support.

To all business owners, you'll likely find that, in most cases, your tax bills are one of the largest expenses your business faces. As hard as you work, tax planning should never be put on the back burner if financial stability is your ultimate goal. For this reason, I highly encourage you to invest time in reading this book. Mastery comes with practice, and by selecting the right tax planner and CPA to guide you, you'll be amazed at how effective tax planning can help you grow your wealth.

Charlene Quah, CPA, CTC

Licensed in Texas State Board and American Institute of Certified Public Accountants, Charlene Quah, is a Houston, TX based CPA and the founder of XQ CPA PLLC, a firm which goes above and beyond in helping business owners to achieve 3 important financial goals: **a)** increase profits **b)** reduce taxes **c)** better manage cash flows. The Firm was incorporated in March of 2012 and in 2024 celebrated its 12th year anniversary.

Charlene possesses more than 20 years of professional experience in public practice including accounting, business management, tax, audit, review, compilation and business consulting. Prior to starting her own firm, she had extensive experience practicing with the Big Four firms and several other mid-sized public accounting firms.

Charlene completed the American Institute for Certified Tax Coaches' inaugural training program leading to the Certified Tax Coach™ designation a decade ago. The Certified Tax Coach™ program focuses on court-tested, IRS-approved tax reduction strategies. Charlene has since developed the Tax Planning 360 program, a Firm methodology and tax planning online tool that has helped hundreds of high-net-worth individuals reduce their tax burden effectively and legally.

Charlene is fluent in several written and spoken languages. She has lived and worked in more than three countries and has earned the CPA designations in all three. She is currently the Partner of XQ CPA PLLC, a firm that goes extra miles to help businesses in increasing profitability, reducing taxes and better manage cash flows. Charlene is also a frequent guest speaker for small business events and conferences.

As the Lead Partner of XQ CPA, Charlene currently leads a team of twenty accountants. At XQ CPA, the team is currently serving more than 500 businesses and mid-sized corporations specializing in accounting, financial management, tax planning and preparation, financial system implementation and business advisory.

In the last 10 years, Charlene has founded two other companies, EpicLedger and OneSelfClub. Epicledger is a technology company that focuses on creating application solutions for businesses. Charlene regularly works with her team of developers and accountants to develop applications for businesses, enabling and empowering businesses to make timely and accurate financial decisions. At Epicledger, new solutions are developed on a quarterly basis. OneSelfClub (OSC) is a service solution provider focusing on delivering accounting services using technology and automation. Clients of OneSelfClub are provided 24/7 adaptive insights to allow real-time financial analysis to be conducted anytime, anywhere. Today, OneSelfClub serves more than 200 active businesses and growing.